— BE —
GOOD
FOR
GOODNESS
SAKE

BY KRISTIN ANDRESS

DEDICATION

For those who truly 'see' others, and in them, see themselves.

Cyndy,
You are a bright
light. Enjoy
each moment.
♡ Kristin

PREFACE

This is OUR World

This is a world where there is peace, and peacefulness.

This is a world where we meet each other where we are.

This is a world where we strive to understand ourselves and others.

This is a world where we do not take counsel in our fears.

This is a world where we ask questions before we judge.

This is a world where the bottom line means working and co-existing together.

This is a world where forgiveness is absolute and history is stuck in its past.

This is a world where every person chooses to step up and do.

This is a world where we choose to take a stand for good, and for each other.

This is a world where the differences of geography, religion, culture and creed cannot compete with pure faith in each other and a higher power.

This is a world of empathy.

This is a world in which we trust, because we are trustworthy.

This is a world where forgiveness heals.

This is a world where we see each other, the real people, behind the masks.

This is a world where posturing and facades are useless.

This is a world where we think for ourselves.

This is a world where we are perpetually in the inquiry of what is possible.

This is a world where we know how to shift perceptions and perspectives to those which serve us, not hurt us.

This is a world where we realize and embrace all that sincere love can do.

This is a world where when bad happens, and it will, we come together in a march of compassion and a quest for acceptance and understanding rather than hate.

This is a world of infinite celebration.

This is a world in which our people, all people, - CAN do and be **GOOD**.

This is a world where we are better hearts, better minds, better to ourselves and others.

Let's see what is real, what is possible.

Let's Be love.
Show love.

Just love.

This is Our World.

THIS IS OUR WORLD!

BE GOOD FOR GOODNESS SAKE

Idyllic. That's what we hope our lives will be, and the world we live in. And, we come to know that that is a bit idealistic. At the same time, why not live each day as best we can…believing it is that good or certainly can be.

So goes the story of being good for goodness sake.

CHAPTER 1

THE CAST

Ray

The rocking chair on the winding porch of the Only Bed and Breakfast on the outskirts of the idle town of Cadence was Ray Jones' favorite place to sit and have a think as he looked out at the old Weeping Willow tree and past it to the rolling meadow that included a hill here and there and part of a cornfield. In the lake beside Old Willow, he often saw his reflection. He liked the soft breeze in the fall and didn't much mind the rain. The cap on his head protected his balding head from the last shimmers of the day.

He was pretty much a resident of this little place and the corresponding small town. People visited for the county fairs, the country cuisine and perhaps a bit of tranquility. It was a place to vacate your real life for a time or placate the one you have or had had. For Ray, his way was the passing of the moments until his actual passing, and it came with the reflection of whether he wasted his life or lived it well over his 80 some years.

Ray watched the arrivals and the departures of the guests. His Host had done the same for over 60 years and he observed her as she stood at the top of the porch steps and looked across the way to the gate straddled by dandelions and cockle burrs and randomly colorful wild flowers … awaiting the arrival of the new batch, ready to introduce their horizon.

The Host certainly saw the stuff of life in the people that slept in her rooms and ate at her table. The comings and goings of dreams, disasters, beliefs, commitments and the downright core of human beings being individuals in a co-created world. Even if she was a spirit of few words, Ray knew that The Host saw the soul of a person as soon as he or she set foot on her soil.

Goodness....we know it when we see it, and we notice when it is missing.

The Alexanders   Alison and Matthew

The Alexander couple, soon to be known as Alison and Matthew (or Matt), arrived midday in what would have been a Cinderella carriage in most fairy tales. In this case, it was a purring luxury SUV projecting the symbolism of wealth. The young Mrs. with crisply cut brown hair stepped out first from the driver's side with an air of impatience and a look of disdain as she scanned the little B&B Ray had grown to love.

Her eyes swept up the ivy along the bricks of the two story cottage for about two shakes prior to marching to the back of the 'wagon' to pull out the luggage before her husband could manage to step a long leg out. He was evidently biding his time while she cursed her cell phone for lack of coverage. Alas, he reluctantly stood by her side.

This was not a place with a concierge or a bellman. There was a struggle with the weight of a large, finely tailored leather bag, but Mrs. Alison Alexander refused her husband's assistance and dropped it on her foot that must have been in pain already in a ludicrously high heel...at least in the countryside. Mr. Matthew Alexander took her elbow, which was immediately pulled away.

She left him to the bags and was greeted by The Host who received nary a thanks when she presented lemonade curtly declined. Mr. Alexander carried the bags up the porch steps and placed them down gently to shake The Host's hand and say 'hello' to Ray before disappearing to the tiff that was obviously already brewing.

Mama Madilyn and Baby Love

It was twilight when the next guests arrived. It is a bewitching hour of beautiful sunsets and much to mystify what might lie in the midst of the waving corn stalks and in the towers of the Weeping Willow, which were no doubt residents of the land or our imaginations. Even in the dusk, the young lady with blonde ponytail atop her head and a simple cotton dress could be seen to have a kind countenance and an excitement of being where she was intended to be. Quickly she took in the surroundings and smiled, mostly to herself. Then she reached into the backseat and out came a baby carrier, with the little one in it asleep. The Host dispatched the aged Ray to help Madilyn with her bags, as the spry Mr. Alexander was already stowed away behind a closed door upstairs.

Madilyn traveled light, thankfully, and Ray placed her bag in a room off the parlor with fireplace (not needed this time of year) before he limped to the foyer to wish the ladies adieu for the evening. It was then that he saw the baby boy was different than his mom….a different color. He also noticed the inquisitive blue eyes gazing back at him. He tipped his cap and promptly excused himself.

With The Host as witness, Madilyn lifted the child and nestled her chin in his curly head, kissed his sweet cheek and accepted with gratitude an evening cocoa.

The Host

All guests present and accounted for and now ready for their rest, The Host set about her evening rituals. First, was to look up at the moon and stars if the heavens permitted it without cloudy skies. Even if she could not see the constellations she could breathe into her lungs the freshness of the earth and appreciate the dew rising from the lake. Then, her task was organizing provisions for sustenance for the morning. Her breakfasts were legendary, as were the scents and smells. In the summer, she titillated senses with flowers from her garden. In the winter, she scintillated appetites with herbs from her greenhouse.

Her table was their table, and it reflected generations. From the wood of an oak, it was 10-feet long and four feet wide. There was but one chair at the head and two long wooden benches at each side. Truly, her guests sat together. That table was notched and marked by those that had dropped knives or forks or simply slapped it with a good laugh or a fist in a moment of realization, leaving an imprint unseen though perhaps remembered. Those marks…were the marks of life. The Host knew she, and her B&B, were but vessels of the journey…and more so, the transition.

The transition? That was her part and parcel of responsibility to the weekend's guests, and those who preceded them. A gentle guide to understanding what it is and means to be good for goodness sake.

The Weeping Willow

Listen to me. Now, I am not just any tree, I am Weeping Willow. I am a character of the story as much as any other, and boy…do I have history. Residing outside the picture window of our little chateau, I have seen the meals partaken among many and from the winding porch, I've listened to the nature of the conversations. At times I know it is good that I cannot speak of the many tales I have witnessed, yet what you will learn is that I do have an influencing voice. Sometimes it is a whisper, so lean in.

You may picture me quite tall, with a trunk so thick many people could stand around me and still perhaps not be able to hold hands to encircle me. My roots go deep and my branches have learned to float with the breeze, with a few falling in the inevitable storms of the seasons. Some of these seasons are reflected in ornaments and artwork that guests have created while here and tied gently to my limbs and branches. The pieces sway gently, grow warm in the sunshine, and reflect the experience of simply taking a moment in time to realize a good thing, and express it however the spirit moves.

In my circle of life, there are many, many rings. We are about to add another with this new assembly of our ground's guests.

Let us listen and let us harvest the goodness.

CHAPTER 2

THE BEGINNING

And so their stories go….

The morning rose in the glimmer of a light rain shower. The drops left the grass and leaves decorated with slivers of diamonds. The fog above the lake spoke to a day of sunshine arriving.

Ray was typically the first to enter the dining area where the miracle of a newspaper would already have appeared. Having no televisions in the place, he did like to keep up on things, meaning the comic section and to heck with the rest.

Today, said newspaper was already in the hands of the high-heeled girl who'd stormed the 'castle' the day before, and who had claimed his high backed chair facing the Weeping Willow and the stalks beyond.

"Mornin'", said Ray. "Pretty day."

Without lowering the paper much her dark eyes glanced quickly over the top and she clipped, "Good morning," and with sarcasm, "Yes, it's raining."

In the entryway, The Host observed her in silence and took in Ray's shrug as Mrs. Alexander returned to the of study her business section of 'his' paper.

Next to arrive was Mr. Alexander. He barreled through the front door in jogging shorts and shoes, and a soaked t-shirt. It was not a quiet arrival as the door banged open with a gust of wind, as he saw the three others before him and grinned widely, "Now that was some run! Man, it is lush out there!" He stepped toward Ray extending his hand, "Hello Sir, I am Matthew Alexander."

Ray took note of the young man's hard grip on his hand, "Well, no Sir required for me, young man. Call me Ray."

"Matt!" Mrs. Alexander scolded as she flipped down the paper and still did not stand in 'hello'. "You are getting rain water everywhere. Take off your shoes. You were not born in a barn!"

Matthew's countenance dropped as he looked down at his dripping on the well-worn hardwood floor. He looked at his wife apologetically, "Alison…" and he was interrupted by The Host.

The Host stepped toward Matthew and gave him a quick hug that imprinted the dew drops on her apron. "No worries on that son. Water dries and", she winked, "Many good people were born in a barn. Perhaps One in particular."

The Host glided toward her kitchen divided from the dining area by a two-way swinging door, through which guests were allowed entry only upon invitation. She began to step through and called over her shoulder. "Alison or Mrs. Alexander if you prefer? Please go see if the little Miss upstairs and the baby are ready to join us. It will be time to break bread together soon."

Alison's jaw dropped at the request.

The Host simply replied, "You cannot expect the men to enter the space of a woman without her permission. It is an appropriate task to ask of you."

The newspaper was thrust toward Matthew who grabbed it and watched his wife hurry up the stairs in a huff. Ray moved to his rightful chair facing the scenery of the Weeping Willow and said, "May I have that please?" He nodded at the crumpled newspaper.

Matthew was bending to take off his shoes and socks and didn't realize he was squeezing the day's news. "Oh yes Sir or Ray I mean." He handed the older gentleman the paper and continued. "Sorry about that. Ally has a lot of responsibility at her work and is stressed out about not having Wi-Fi out here or access to a workable cell phone carrier."

Ray harrumphed. "If that stuff was here, I'd be taking my leave. This is a place to just be." He paused as he heard the young man before him breathe deeply. "Now, you better go get yourself dried off. You are about to experience the best breakfast on earth." His wrinkled face and cloudy blue eyes looked up at young Matthew, and Ray smiled.

Matthew smiled back, though Ray saw in his clear blue, the sadness, before he turned to jog up the stairs.

In that moment, Ray as well as the Weeping Willow, knew that Matthew was in the right place, and probably at the right time.

Alison (Mrs. Alexander)

She was a cussing person, but mostly inside her head. Alison sat at boardrooms and bars with the best of the best in her profession and new what it meant to continuously swim upstream. As a woman, she was as good as her last success and was hardcore to the core. And, here she was in a dim hallway at an Only B&B in the middle of wherever, at the door of a stranger, ready to knock.

Knock she did and the person within called out, "Just a minute!! Be right there."

Alison tapped a toe, which was enclosed in a finely designed leather sandal. She'd packed her semblance of 'country wear'. She sighed heavily, loudly.

The door swung open and the bright face of a much shorter, very thin, 20-something girl with a baby on her hip filled the opening. In a rush of words she spurted, "Oh hello! I am so running late. You were sent for me? Thank you! Can you give me a hand? Please come in." She had already turned into her room and Alison hesitantly stepped in. "Here, can you just hold him for a minute while I get his carrier ready?"

A baby was thrust into Alison's hands. "Oh! Oh..well...no."

"Don't worry. He is old enough to hold his head up without your support. Eight months. Just little. Just a sec. I need to find my flip flops and his blanket. Beautiful rain outside, but I don't want him to get cold."

Alison found herself holding her arms out straight with a baby between her hands. She looked at it, and audibly gasped. He was black. The girl was white. Her next thought, "How was the girl so thin. Could a person lose baby weight that fast?"

Madilyn and Baby Braylon

Madilyn slipped on her thread bare flips and blew out a breath as she maneuvered around a small daybed to the lady holding her baby. She saw her for the first time and the stiffness which she held the small life before her. "Sorry about that. Still pretty new to me figuring out how to take care of both of us."

The lady held the baby toward her and Madilyn naturally replaced him on her hip. She extended her free hand, "Hi. I am Madilyn. And, this little guy is Braylon. Guess we will be sharing a home for a few days, huh?" She smiled and closed her mouth quickly as she noticed the woman eyeballing her teeth. They were not completely even. She knew, but her mouth did not obey and she smiled yet again, "What is your name?"

The woman took a moment, seemingly unglued. "Oh, I am Alison. Alison Alexander. I am at this wretched place in the middle of nowhere at the insistence of my husband Matt." She rolled her eyes.

"Nice to meet you Alison. So, you don't like the place? Seems idyllic to me."

"I'm sure." Alison gave Madilyn a quick head to toe and nearly scoffed aloud at her frayed jeans and stained pull over sweatshirt. "Shall we go downstairs?" Alison hurried toward the door.

Madilyn took another deep breath. Judgement from others was certainly not her first rodeo. She kissed Braylon and smiled. For now, they were here and she found it lovely.

Breaking Bread

Madilyn carried Braylon slowly down the stairs, still sometimes afraid he would break. She entered the dining area several steps behind the harried Alison, and as she saw the high chair awaiting she called a relieved thank you to The Host. As if prompted, The Host entered through her swinging kitchen door carrying dishes of aromatic food.

"Oh, can I help you in there?" Madilyn asked.

In reply The Host said, "I believe you have your hands full.' She looked over Madilyn's shoulder to the living room where the Alexanders stood with backs toward Ray and his paper in a quiet but animated discussion. The Host called, "Matthew, my dear, will you please lend a hand?"

Matthew quickly stepped away from his wife and locked eyes with The Host, "Absolutely, what can I do?"

"You can serve. Come with me." And, Matthew was allowed entry through the swinging door to the mysteries of the kitchen within. He emerged moments later with baskets of breads, and again, his grin. A grin that disclosed he had experienced…well, something.

As he placed the dishes, Madilyn settled the baby in the high chair. Matthew looked at the baby and then Madilyn, taking in their difference, and then reached out a hand to Madilyn. "Hi there. I am Matthew or Matt, and who is this little guy?" He knelt beside the high chair and took his little hand softly.

"This is the most amazing boy ever. His name is Braylon. And, I am Madilyn or well, my sister called me Madi."

"Well, Madi. He is beautiful. How old is Braylon?"

"Well, Matthew," she smiled as she pronounced his full first name, "He is 8 months old, and thank you. I think he is a gift and a gem."

Ray entered the room and took in the scene of Matthew on his knee by the child and his wife looking on from a distance with perplexed contempt. Oh, what a weekend it would be. He knew.

The Host re-entered the dining space and opened her arms to indicate they should be seated. She took the only seat at the head of the table, closest to the kitchen. Ray and Matthew perched on one side of the benches, the ladies on the other. After a brief moment of silence wherein some bowed heads and others observed, The Host passed the first dish.

The Weeping Willow beyond the picture window danced in the continuing breeze and looked on.

Matthew started the conversation. "Now, this is some spread! When I've been at B&B's before, it's really been continental. You grab a plate and get your food. Nice to have a sit down and pass around, eh Ally?"

Ally shrugged as she quickly passed on fried potatoes and the bacon to

Ray who sat directly across from her. Ray said, "We don't go hungry here, but Mrs. Alexander, if you don't put anything on your plate you certainly will!" He laughed and Madi and The Host joined him. Matthew darted a nervous gaze across the table to his wife.

Ally swallowed a drink of water and then said, "Well, I see there is fruit on its way around and some scrambled eggs."

"The bread here is to live for," Ray offered. "All kinds of it and I still don't know what the marmalades are made of or if the butter comes directly from the cows next door."

"Butter?" Alison cleared her throat and took a quick glance at Ray's little pot belly just over the belt on his pants. "I tend to watch my carbs."

"Doesn't seem this little one does!" Ray guffawed as he watched Madilyn splay a spoonful or so of every dish or basket passed her way.

Madilyn put her hand over her mouth that had just taken a quick bite and her eyes were wide. She swallowed and said, "My goodness, I know. I have a hollow leg as my grandma used to say. But this is heaven! And it all smells so good. Thank you for preparing this," she gleamed as she acknowledged The Host who nodded with delight.

Matthew was smiling directly at the baby as he stated, "I imagine with little Braylon you have to keep up your energy."

Madilyn nodded and giggled as she put her hand on Braylon's cheek. "He is such a good boy, but I'm just figuring it all out. It's wild to witness his personality and his…"

Alison interrupted and asked sardonically, "Really, what kind of name is *Braylon?*"

It sounded to Ray like that was not an inquiry, but an accusation. He put down his fork and looked at that woman with concern.

Madilyn was good and responded quickly. "Thank you for asking. It is an important name. As you can see, no doubt, his father was African American. His name was Lonnie and he was an athlete and a scholar." She paused. "His mother's name was unconventional as well. It was Braidy, even spelled funny too. So, when baby boy was born, they named him Braylon. I looked up the actual meaning and it is associated with giving back. Perhaps he will be our next famous humanitarian!"

Madilyn tickled him and Braylon giggled, and his beautiful hazel eyes stayed put on Alison as he did so. She turned away.

Ray heard the crickets chirping in the ensuing silence, until he intuitively felt The Host seeking his role as elder. "Well, so…you are not Braylon's mom?"

"I am his aunt, and now I'm his mom. I was his godmother so Braylon was given to me two months ago upon the passing of my sister and brother in law, his parents, in a random car crash." She bowed her head through a waft of grief before looking around the table with glimmering eyes. "Sorry for the downer, but there is really no bad day with this little guy lighting my life."

Matthew piped up, but quietly. "Not a downer, Madi. Thank you for sharing and for doing what you are doing. I'm sure it is a lot to deal with and to take on."

"Matthew, my little Braylon is teaching me more than my college classes could have ever…"

"*You* go to college?" Alison asked in surprise, interrupting Madilyn yet again.

"Ally!" Matt sighed putting his hand on his forehead.

"What? I'm just asking!" Alison leveled him.

Ray cleared his throat. "Well Miss Madilyn. I believe Braylon and I may need to have to have a ride on the porch swing a little later. Maybe we can take our naps at the same time."

Madilyn nodded and The Host laughed, while Matthew regrouped and asked, "Sir…Ray, if I may ask, what was your profession?"

"Military, son, and I would imagine you either grew up in the South with the use of sir, or you may have an experience there too?"

Matthew swallowed his bite of quiche, "Yes to both, actually. I was in law school, but when the war started, I enlisted and was deployed."

Alison fumed, "We were just married at that time and he could have had a very lucrative career, but no. That's my job."

"Thank you for your service. Both of you," Madilyn interjected. "Ray, Vietnam?"

"Yes ma'am, Miss Madi. My son and two daughters missed out a bit or perhaps I should say I did, as I was not home often in their younger years. Once I got out I had to figure out how to go on, but the best thing you can do is love them the best you can I guess. Sometimes I wonder if I could have done it better."

After a brief silence Madilyn chimed in again and quietly said, "My mom used to say to my sister and me that you do the best you can with what you know."

"Amen," The Host said and stood. "I believe everyone is finished for now, as is the rain. Perhaps you will take a stroll or sit on the porch. After we serve there is much to be seen. Much to be said. Much to be thought about. Much good to be. And, much good to do."

Ray chuckled and slapped the table as he scooted his chair back, "Now, you all get used to that. The Host says that at the end of every meal."

Breakfast concluded, but many thoughts hovered with the lingering sense of pending revelations. The Host declined Madilyn and Matthew's offers to clear the table and with a steady tone and enunciated, "You", she said, "You, deserved to be served."

CHAPTER 3

ONLY A DAY

The Day's Adventure

Ray's Day

Well that was some first breaking of bread together. As always, The Host has congregated an interesting bunch. What the world will hold for each is sure to be an adventure.

Adventure for me is that porch swing, a good book, and a snooze. A good chat of telling tales or debating politics with a guest is also welcome. Primarily, like the Weeping Willow, I am an observer, but I do have a voice and sometimes have my say.

I could sum up the parts of those who visited the Only Bed & Breakfast in one word…complicated. At my age, I am aware life was never to go in a straight line. Nope. It zigged and it zagged and it ebbed and it flowed. That's the stuff that makes us who we are and our decisions about approaching the good, bad or flat out ugly are what make our perceptions and perspectives ours to own. You see, we are going to be dealt a hand that's outside of our control. We are also going to be dealt a playing field on which to create what we try to. In that creating, sometimes it works out. Sometimes it doesn't. Still, we have the choice to see it as we will.

The Weeping Willow

I look at Ray each day. I see him clearly.

Over his time on that porch swing he has swung forward and he swung backward. He saw what could still be and he saw what would never be. It's impossible to reinvent our own history, but the days forward....well, that can be something to think about. With the wisdom of his years and the experiences of his lifetime, Ray's decision was to listen, learn and every so often serve as a sage in giving a nugget of advice. He decided the guests, should they choose to swing with him, might just get a sentence or two or even an earful depending.

Matthew Alexander was the first to sit beside him. That's coming soon....

Matthew and Alison - Just Another Day

Uncharacteristically, Matthew did not bound outside after that bountiful breakfast to enjoy the peace of the surroundings he craved. He sat on the edge of the bed replaying his latest battle with his wife.

"Matt! This is ridiculous. We have nothing in common with these people! I am so ready to go."

"Ally, we just got here."

"Exactly, and I'm bored, getting behind, cannot even be in contact with the real world. Besides, you pay more attention to that kid and its mom (air quotes) than you do to me."

"Seriously, Ally? Seriously?"

"Yes, seriously. I'm seriously sick of this God forsaken place. I'm leaving and finding a place to log in. See you later."

In his mind's eye, Matthew recalled Alison lurching to her feet, grabbing her laptop and the car keys and hurrying out the bedroom door and down the stairs. At least she had not slammed the door and embarrassed him further.

And…he did not follow.

Ray and Matthew…and Honor

Matthew walked onto the porch leisurely with t-shirt, shorts, bare feet and with a book in hand. He was headed down the short set of steps to the cool grass, now dry from the warm sun and breeze to the shade of the Weeping Willow.

"Well, hello, young Matthew, whatcha reading there?"

"Oh, Ray. Sorry, didn't see you there." He was distracted, still thinking of Ally who had careened off in the SUV to find a cyber café somewhere in the next town.

"Have a seat, son." Ray halted the movement of his painted white swing and patted the place beside him. Matt sat and they resumed swinging gently, back and forth, back and forth. Matt's gaze stayed focused on the giant tree, and the silence was not broken for a time.

Matt stirred and glanced at the elder gentleman, "How long you been here, Ray?"

"Took me about 78 years to get here. It's a long journey to know home, Matthew."

Matt nodded and with hesitation, "If I may ask, what was the Vietnam experience?"

"You may ask, but I may not answer. I came back roughed up inside and out. Marriage went south. Kids were still pretty young when we split, and I'd split mentally too. Took me a long time to realize what was important. It certainly wasn't money or prestige. I may have won the Congressional Medal of Honor, but…"

"Wait! You won the CMH? Wow, what did you…"

Ray raised a hand. "Hold on young fellow. That medal is important as I served my country, but the real award is in how you step up in your life. You do not get a medal for being a good father or a good parent, a good son or a good daughter. Those are badges of honor that are often overlooked and forgotten."

Matthew shook his head. "I may not know the joy of fatherhood. Ally doesn't want kids. Says it will interfere with her career path."

"And, soldier, what do you want?" Ray asked keeping his face forward to watch the Weeping Willow sway.

"Well….I want…."

They were interrupted by Madi and Braylon bursting onto the front porch with a blast of energy. "Hi! Sorry, did I interrupt? Oh my gosh! Isn't that the most beautiful sound you have ever heard!" She swished her free arm toward the Weeping Willow with its magical ornaments left by patrons of past, and sometimes joining together in the breeze, sounding like bells or chimes.

Matt listened. He had not heard the whispers until now.

Madi tilted her head as she noticed their reverie. "Ray? How about I take you up on that offer of holding on to Braylon while Matt and I go have a look out there? I want to see what really creates this beautiful voice in the wind!" In a yellow prairie skirt and pink tank top, and the charming ponytail atop her head, she moved to the front of the swing, passed Braylon to Ray and grabbed Matt's hand, pulling him down the stairs and into the grass where she kicked off her flip flops and ran toward the tree, Matt in tow.

Now that girl had energy….or call it gumption.

Weeping Willow...I See You

Here they come, the first two in my embrace of branches. The girl with the smile hiding grief stricken eyes and a fear-filled heart, and the boy who has seen and experienced too much and looks lost. That's how I saw them through the window at the first breakfast.

They stepped under my willow branches and touched some of the ornaments, wondering what each represented. This I knew, but could not say. Most of them make up their own stories before they realize the need to create their own.

My foundation is set, but my limbs move and I touch my people at every given chance as they walk within my cloak of leaves.

Matthew and Madi

There was so much to see, so many stories told or untold under the Willow. Some old. Some new. Some tried. Some true. Reflections all, of who we are.

"Matthew! Come look at this one! It is a crystal. See how it catches the sunshine when it can get through the branches?"

Matt stepped closer to have a look. "Oh yeah, that's pretty. I think the person that hung that was going in circles and trying to find a straight path."

Madi laughed, "Yes, and for this one that looks like a mini-bird feeder, perhaps she could not feed her soul enough and needed the wings of others."

"Good one!" They circled the trunk of the tree looking at the Weeping Willow's keepsakes. Talking all the time until Matt stopped when the circle was complete.

"Madi? Why do you always call me Matthew? Most call me Matt."

She tilted her head and raised her shoulders in a shrug. "Well, on the first day you gave me two choices Matthew or Matt. Matthew suits you better."

"Really? How so?"

Madi shifted her bare feet in the grass. "Matthew is a strong name and I see that within you. It's obvious you have overcome some stuff in life." She waited for his response.

"I was adopted when I was five." He bent his head, not intending to be so personal so fast.

"Ah, there you go. You are a survivor and I bet you are creative, as well as complicated. You want to please in order to be loved, and you have a mind of your own that leads you to see the good in all people and fast. I saw that you saw that in Braylon."

"And in you, Madi. Thank you," he pushed a branch out of the way so he could look at her squarely, "Where the heck you getting all these words to say to me?" He shrugged and raised his hands in wonder.

"Don't you know? This tree speaks! He is whispering them in my ear!" They looked up and laughed aloud together before Madi took Matthew's hand and looked him in his clear blue eyes. "And, Matthew, you are certainly not intended to be a door mat."

With that they heard the crunch of tires rolling fast across gravel and saw the dazzling now dust covered SUV, flying up the path and coming to a quick halt before the Only B&B. The next sound was a slamming door.

Matthew and Madi reluctantly released clasped hands. Matt paused and touched his forehead and palms to the trunk of the Weeping Willow. "Thank you, old man. Thank you, Madi", he whispered.

Matthew poofed out a quick breath of air and then turned away to stroll toward his waiting wife whose arms crossed her chest as she stared him down.

He thought he heard from behind a soft voice saying, "You are welcome. Thank you too, Mattie."

Ally and Matt

Matthew appraised his wife as he walked from beneath the Willow branches to the graveled path road. She was beautiful and always put together as people often said. She worked at being good at all she did.

"Hi there! How was…"

"Well, that looked pretty cozy," Alison said in greeting.

Ignoring the snide remark, Matthew asked, "Did you find a cyber-café? Get done what you wanted to? You've missed a really beautiful day here."

"There is nothing to do here, Matt."

Matt merely shrugged. "There is for me." And, he slowly walked away.

The Weeping Willow

I didn't like to see my Mattie and Madi move away from me. That was a display of innocent love. Two people really seeing each other, and becoming friends in acceptance and even confusion. The blossom of friendship is not indicative of romance. It is deep ceded in pure intention…the intention of which is to simply show you care. They do not call me a Weeping Willow for nothing. If I had tears, they would have anointed those kids' heads. Healing happens when people say what needs said and it is heard and held close. That is a beginning, right there. I know.

Madi and Ray

Madi's heart hurt for Matt as she witnessed the reception of his wife, but she smiled up at the tree and jogged back toward the porch, snatching her flip flops in the grass and bounded up the steps to sit by Ray who had Braylon against his chest, head on broad shoulder, sound asleep.

Madi touched Braylon's soft cheek. "He's a good little guy, huh? I hope I am enough to fill his heart someday," she said as she thought of Matthew's journey of adoption and what must have been such a transition to a new home and parents. She repositioned herself with one knee up on the swing to face Ray and Braylon. "Ray, may I ask you something?"

"Sure, Miss Madi. Shoot," he said quietly, caressing the back of Braylon's head and breathing in his curly hair.

She cleared her throat. "Has it been hard for you?"

Ray's lips curved into a small smile and he glanced at her petite frame beside his. "Do you mean has it been hard for me to be a Black man?"

Madi put her hand on his elbow and squeezed, feet still swinging above the porch floor. "Oh Ray, I didn't mean…"

"No, no little one. It's quite okay and a good question. The answer is, 'yes', it has been tough for me on occasion." He paused.

A short sigh and she said quietly, "I am really sorry about that."

"Why? What did you have to do with it? You weren't even born when some of that stuff happened. Yes, Miss Madi, the hardship of my life sometimes did have to do with the color of my skin, but it more often had to do with myself. See, there were times of good decision and bad decision, especially where my wife and family were concerned. I didn't like myself much and therefore, they didn't much like me either. I disappeared in a wilderness of anger and self-destruction, and I lost the love in my life because of it. It does not take the color of skin to cause that to happen to ourselves. It doesn't take whether we are rich or we are poor. Man or woman. It just takes us figuring out how to be in the world."

With hesitation, Madi continued, "So, how did you move on or change or…."

He put his big, well-groomed fingers on her hand. "I simply decided that today is a new day and I wanted to be good, feel good and do good. It is as easy as a choice and a thought." He cleared his throat. "Now, you are asking me this because you are raising a black child."

"I love him so much. I want everything for him."

"Of course you do. You are a mother." He knew she had tears on her cheeks though he kept his eyes focused on the tree. "Know this though, you guide him well and you let him be him. What 'everything' is to him, may be different than what it is for you. And that's okay. That's what makes this big ol' world go round. Our differences and our similarities." He reached in his pocket and gave her his handkerchief. "If you want my opinion, he will be a-okay. He has you, doesn't he? And, Madi, your sister would be proud."

Madi hugged Ray hard and didn't let go until Braylon lifted his head and smiled at them, causing them to laugh together and continue to swing before Madi asked, "Ray, do you like yourself today?"

His shoulders rose and fell, "I sure do today, Miss Madi. And, that's all we got right now."

CHAPTER 4

THE NEXT DAY

Ray and Alison

The next day, Ray meandered with "his" newspaper under his arm onto the porch as dawn was breaking. He was not surprised to find Alison sitting on his swing, staring off into the field and lake beyond the Weeping Willow. There was a notepad beside her, but it was empty. This was Ray's favorite time of day just before breakfast together and he was curious to find what would she "be" in the coming moments? An interloper or a friend?

"Mornin' again, Alison."

She jumped. "Oh! Good morning, Ray. Sorry, I didn't hear you."

Ray was aware the door to the porch creeks a good bit when it opens, but when a person is in faraway land, a lot can go unnoticed. "This is one of my favorite times of day. May I?" He pointed to the swing on which she was sitting in the middle.

She scooted to the side, "Yes, of course."

Ray sat and the silence ensued. Alas, he said, "Alison, when most people sit and swing with me they tend to ask questions. Since you are not, allow me one of my own please."

Her jaw clenched and she looked over at him with reluctance. "Okay."

"What are you doing here?"

"I was just enjoying the morning air…"

Ray put up a hand, "No. No. You know that is not what I mean. What are you doing *here*?" He spread his hands to the landscape.

Alison pursed her lips and shook her head as if waving off the emotion of caring.

"Come, girl. The truth *can* set you free."

Alison smirked, "Well, if you must know, our counselor suggested it."

"Marriage counselor, then?"

She nodded as the breeze spoke, and a wisp of her cropped hair, stuck on her lip. Ray wanted to reach out his hand to move it away. She looked so young, so vulnerable, and yet so like a twig ready to snap. He gave her the moments of quiet necessary to form her voice. He pushed the swing back with his feet and rested his arms over his hungry belly, waiting for her to say…

"You see, Ray, I don't want children. Matt does. I want my career and travel and to see the world. I want a partner who carries his own weight financially and has ambition."

"I see."

"I don't know how to get him to change."

Without a second of pause, Ray smacked his leg and let out a guffaw.

Alison bristled, "What!?"

Ray turned to her and put his arm on the back of the swing, lightly grazing her tense back. "Ally girl, you cannot change people. No matter how much you want to, we can only do that for ourselves. You gotta let Matthew be Matthew. Let you be you. And, if you can meet somewhere in the middle on that then you will be just fine. If you cannot, paths will part and you will make your own way."

Alison glared at him searching for words, and as Ray kept her in the present of that moment, she slowly leaned back on his arm, her cool neck covering his brown skin, perhaps sensing and needing his internal and eternal strength.

After a little bit of that quiet and pause she asked, "How do I do that?"

"Now, if I had that answer I'd probably be a very rich man though I'm not sure I'd be a happy one. One thing I do know is you have to talk. You have to listen. You have to postpone judgement, especially until you get your facts. And, you have to ask questions. You just asked a good one and that's a start."

She breathed so deeply he could see her ribcage through her thin blouse. She blew out the breath and her eyes closed momentarily, perhaps squinting back a tear she typically refused to show. Ray knew…the tough, typically are not so tough.

Ray broke the silence again, "I do have another question for you. That okay?"

She angled her heart shaped face to look at him, one dimple appearing in an unspoken 'okay'.

"Why do you not want to have kids?"

Alison sat upright her hands on her knee with a straight on view of the Weeping Willow sashaying in another morning breeze. She tilted her head. Did she hear a wind chime? "I'll say it fast and please don't repeat it, Ray. I know I can tell you because I will never see you again."

He crossed his heart and smiled upward, but her eyes were on the Willow.

"I grew up quite poor." She put her hand up as if to halt the next question he had no intention of asking. "I know. I know. I don't act it and I do hide it. My parents divorced when I was five. I had two big brothers. My parents didn't argue in front of us post-divorce, and we didn't even know we didn't have much until later. Then, I began seeing it – all that was missing and the teasing that came with it. And, the men in my life – related or otherwise – always let me down. So, I made a decision. I've busted my tail to get to where I am through pursuing my education, working crazy long hours, climbing up with promotions, shouldering a ton of responsibility, and I'm hell bent on ensuring I'm not off loaded because of maternity leave and the perception of motherhood in the workforce. Besides, I can't see bringing a child into *this* world."

Ray nodded, heard the voice of the Weeping Willow sweep through the porch, and then he took a risk. He stopped the swing and took her face in his big hands, and felt that which was soft through her hardness. "I get that, sweet Alison. I do. I may have even been there and done that, just on a different path. But, what I don't want for you is to repeat what I did and that boiled down to not knowing what is really important. I mean really important, and not by anyone else's standards, but by your own. It isn't *this* world you refer to, it is *our* world."

Her eyes were wide and she blinked until alas, Ray released her face, but not before wiping a phantom tear from her cheek. She cleared her throat, "Sorry. I don't usually…"

"You will be okay, Ally. If you let yourself be. Don't reach my age, and wonder where it all went before then. Deal?" Ray pushed with his feet and the swing rocked back and forth on that great porch. The Weeping Willow rocked with them.

Alas, Ally lifted her journal, stood, and finally said, ""Why do you think people put those things on the tree?"

"Now Alison, that is a very good question. Another very good start."

She gave Ray's hand a pat before removing herself to enter the Only B&B.

Ray followed, ready to explore the amazing aromas of their next feast.

The Weeping Willow

That was a good talk, maybe one of the best, but what I do know is that one good talk does not an understanding make. It does, however, make a dent in realizing one's human needs and that whatever that is it is perfect, because it is you. And, an opening is created when we open up to one another. It is good to know there is safety in roots, branches and seeds.

The Host

The Host had prepared breakfast in the hidden kitchen and stepped beyond the swinging doors to bear witness to her guests' interactions.

Braylon was toying with his dry cereal as Ray played with him, laughing as he smacked the high chair tray in front of him making the cereal pieces bounce and laughing harder when Braylon squealed with delight.

Matthew and Madi were sitting side by side animatedly discussing their love of art and their favorite paintings and museums.

Alison entered from the upper level in black designer running gear and stopped short, quickly taking in the interactions

Matt stood. "Hey, Ally, going for a run? I got one in early, but can change after breakfast to…."

"I think I'll take this one alone." She hesitated, "Maybe see some of the property."

"Sure. There are some awesome trails by the lake over there," he waved a hand and trailed off as he lost her attention a she moved toward the table.

Ally glanced at Madi as she took her seat across from Matt. "Did I hear you guys talking about art?"

"Yeah, turns out Madi is a bit of a connoisseur!" Ray piped in.

Alison frowned, "Really? How so?" She crossed her arms, her usual defense.

Madi smiled at her, "I know. Doesn't seem like it, huh? But, the first two paintings I probably saw were a Picasso and a Rembrandt."

"School trip to a museum?" Alison said snidely, and Ray gave her a look.

The pitying look Madi gave to Alison said what needed to be said. "Oh no, Alison. They were but two of the paintings in my father's library when I was growing up. The rest of the estate had lovely pieces by Da Vinci, Renoir, or Van Gogh. He mostly loaned them to galleries and museums though. My favorite was the one I painted at age 10 that was framed and put above his desk in his office. I haven't seen it in some time or him for that matter." Madi turned her attention and smile to Braylon who was enjoying holding onto a spoon and one of Ray's fingers.

The Host noted that there was no boasting. Madi's revelation was quite matter of fact. As a matter of fact, she looked uneasy and wistful. It was a first mention of her own father.

Alison was flustered, "But then, um, why…." She waved her hand and spilled her small glass of juice. "I'm so sorry! Let me clean…"

Madi leaped to her feet to dry the juice with her napkin before it spilled onto Alison. Quickly she chirped, "Happens all the time. Braylon spills daily and…."

The Host interrupted. "Mary? Will you kindly help me in the kitchen?"

Madi stopped what she was doing and turned toward The Host who was observing her. "Oh? Me?" Madi's eyes widened as the kitchen held a mysterious meaning of entering by invitation only. "Of course. However," she bit her lip, "my name is Madilyn."

The Host smiled and the sunshine came through the window highlighting the Weeping Willows' full view of the guests. "Yes. I know. Come. After we serve there is much to be seen. Much to be said. Much to be thought about. Much good to be. And, much good to do."

They entered through the swinging door and emerged minutes later with Madi's face serene, and the delights of the day before them.

The Weeping Willow

Well now isn't that a gas? The good one was wealthy and the seemingly not so good one was not. Life really is a stage, isn't it? And, there is much in a name. The Host could have meant 'merry', because Madi certainly is at least that on the surface. She vibrates with worry on the inside. And yet, Madilyn, is a derivative name of the one and only Mary Magdalene. Madi's serenity came upon entering the kitchen and her smile lit up upon seeing her son. Hmmm…

I see what people show me. And, I also intuit what they do not. The intention is to bear witness as people appear. With them and also with you, the true you always emerges.

Alison and Madilyn and Braylon

Alison spread a blanket under the tree. She returned Ray's wave as he floated on his swing and then lay on her tummy with book in hand. Reading…she hadn't read a novel in quite a while. She had her notepad with her, but it was still empty since with no reception she had no calls for which to take notes. She had just read her first three pages, three times, when Madi's bare feet appeared beside her and then, baby Braylon on the grass before her.

She sat up abruptly.

"Hi! Whatcha readin'?" Madi plopped beside Braylon who was busy pulling at the grass and making giggly noise.

Alison looked at Madilyn in confusion, "Did you need something?"

"Oh, no. We just like this tree. Do you ever wonder what he would say if he could talk?"

Alison scrunched her forehead and then decided to play along. "Well, what if he is a she?"

Madi laughed, "Good point. She would probably have a different slant on the story."

"Right." Alison caught a quick glimpse of Ray's chin lifting and his eyes on her from the swing. "Well, he or she would have a lot to say."

Madi tickled Braylon who held out pieces of grass to Alison.

Alison gingerly took the blade of grass and quietly said, "Thank you." Her eyes rest on Braylon as she asked, "Madi, do you want your own kids?"

Madi shifted to sit with her legs crossed over one another. "Ally, this *is* my kid. He may have been a gift, but he is mine. Do I someday want to actually birth a child? I don't know. If love comes into my life, may-be. There are also a lot of them who just need a home so perhaps I can do more good that way. I'm young enough to let it unfold."

Alison nodded and quickly stated, "I am sorry about your sister. I really am." She started to touch Madi's knee and quickly retracted her hand.

"Thank you. I miss her," she glanced upward, "But, I'm so pleased I have Braylon to remind me of her daily."

"I'd think it would be hard to be reminded."

"No. It is actually beautiful. In all of us, in some way, a piece of us lives on. I guess it comes down to a matter of what we want that to be."

Alison pointed to her useless phone, "It's easier to say that when away from reality."

"Maybe." Madi grabbed for Braylon as he reached for Ally's hair. "Oh! Sorry. He's so curious."

Alison smiled. "Come here little guy." She lifted him in the air and he squealed in delight. She stood him on unbalanced little toes and held on. "He'll be walking before you know it."

"Yes." Madi just watched a natural who didn't know it and who may never know it.

Alison's gaze drew over Madi's shoulder to Matt leaning on the doorway, watching on. Was that a look of hope? She wasn't sure she could cultivate that. It is his life too.

"You know, Madi, I may not want kids of my own. I don't know yet. But, it doesn't mean I can't like others' kids."

Madi kissed Braylon's cheek. "Or love them."

They sat quietly watching Braylon enjoy the cool of the shade and the simple fun of the grass in his hands. Eventually, Alison asked, "Madi? Who do you suppose The Host is?"

Madi shrugged. "I suppose whoever we want her to be."

They laughed together and from his swing, Ray listened and he smiled.

Weeping Willow

It really is okay to be who you are. Whoever that may be. The discovery is up to you. Your fundamental gift to yourself and to others is simply love. Below my branches are two very different people with common concerns in the world. What will happen? Who am I? What is right? Will all be okay? These elements are the essence of connection. It is our willingness and our ability to seek and to see that generates the goodness of being.

CHAPTER 5

THE LAST BREAKFAST

All guests are at the big table again.

After a step of hesitation, The Host motioned to Alison to follow her into the kitchen. Alison was bewildered and a look of fear and skepticism crossed her face. She glanced at Matt, who nodded her on.

Alison stepped through the swinging door and stopped in her tracks. It was not the kitchen of an old B&B. It was modern, with new appliances and all of the accoutrements a wonderful cook could ever want. The ceiling was higher than the dining area, but how was that possible? The lighting came from everywhere and above. It was what she wanted to see.

Alison stood still looking around and feeling uncomfortable. "Should I start here?" She referred to the island with pans of steaming sausages, eggs, muffins, bacon, toast, gravy, oatmeal, potatoes, fresh fruit…a feast prepared to deliver to the guests. Ally reached for a blueberry, pulled back and popped a small piece of muffin in her mouth. She closed her eyes a moment to savor the flavor.

The Host approached her slowly and put a hand on her heart and another on her head then took a step back to meet her eyes. The Host smiled at Ally, "It is good. It just needs to bake. Let's take a minute in here to allow that."

They sat on two stools at an island in silence. Ally felt a warmth rising within. It was acceptance. Resisting the urge to snag a piece of bacon she said to The Host, "I am sorry I spilled my juice."

The Host grasped her shoulder, shook her and laughed. "Dear, it is about time you did. Now, shall we?" She nodded at the still steaming food.

They emerged together with dishes on platters and scents and sense experienced over the few days that would stick to their memories for a lifetime.

The Host asked Ally to spoon biscuits and gravy onto each guest's plate.

And, Ally served.

After which…The Host said, "Now, there is much to be seen. Much to be said. Much to be thought about. Much good to be. Much good to do."

Departing Ray

Together, we typically watch each guest leave from our perches on the porch, The Host in the front and me to the right side on my swing. It is a melancholy day as the guests transition to their lives and away from the sanctuary of stillness and reflection. Some have had distinct realizations. Some have challenges in process. Some have pending decisions. All have been moved.

We witnessed Alison and Matt at their symbolic SUV bump into each other on the driver's side, and after a moment of closeness, Ally gave Matthew the keys.

We enveloped Madi as she hugged each of us with Braylon on her side, and cried happy tears as a car arrived for her from town, at her father's request. Not a taxi this time, but a sedan offering a ride to see Braylon's grandfather.

Braylon chose his other Grandpapa…in Ray, well, me. As it goes with old souls, the two of us locked eyes and gave kisses knowing we knew one another before…and would after.

"Here we are on the swing again," thought Ray as he watched the last particles of dust settle from the cars' departures. "Well, Weeping Willow, you gave me more again, didn't you? I wonder what will you whisper this time? What gifts might you give? Whose heart might you heal? What I do know is that in these past few days, I have certainly received." Ray smiled and closed his eyes.

Through The Host's Eyes

On the horizon, The Host saw the next vehicle approach with passenger or passengers within who were about to discover…well, discover what? The Host knew they would discover what they were going to discover in days when it is time. She would see them, and life would see them through. The idea was to have them truly see each other.

Often, The Host was asked why the name, The Only B&B. A few guests thought that sounded lonely. A few felt it was exclusive. It's all in the way you see a life. You get only one of those or at least one at a time. It might be solitary, though it is not exactly necessary to feel that way. It is certainly individual. And, never simple. It is only yours….to choose.

In my mind's eye, I choose to see you for you. That, my guests, is the epitome of goodness.

Our Only blessing is that you recognize that good begets good. So be good for goodness sake.

The Weeping Willow

They left me gifts. Every guest does. And they reap their own gifts.

Their ornaments are of the every kind. Sometimes they are depicted in a memento or memorabilia representing the meaning of their experience of the Only B&B. Other times they are in the form of hug, touch, tears or talk.

The sweet little one with grief and fear-filled eyes received the goodness of calm acceptance and renewed confidence. She knows she is never alone as she raises the sun for others while raising a son.

The lost boy with the fit exterior received the goodness of a renewed will to find the right way for him, and the understanding that he can be loyal, while also being decidedly strong.

The woman with a hardened heart has a journey ahead and much to realize before she understands and accepts that her perspective and behaviors are the true basis of reaping true life success.

Baby love Braylon received the goodness of love by many, and the imprint of knowing how to pass it on. He will have many, many years to do so.

Carry On

The Weeping Willow…will always offer a canopy for trust and truth.

Ray….will always be sunshine.

The Host….will always serve.

It's time to begin…again and again.

Remember that after we serve there is much to be seen.

Much to be said.

Much to be thought about.

Much good to be.

Much good to do.

And…..that is good.

Be Good for Goodness Sake.

ACKNOWLEDGEMENTS

My mom raised me to see the good in people, typically no matter what they did or how they looked or who they were, where they lived or the nature of their past. For this, I am grateful to have learned to see the inside as the most important reflection of humanity. She is my Host, My Weeping Willow and my Ray.

To my dad, who passed away before this was published, you were often in my thinking of what to say and not say or do and not do. As a little girl until your final breath my intention was to please you. I hope I have done so.

To my brother, the obvious is that I'll always be smarter than you. (Yes, I know he is reading this and laughing.) I respect your capabilities and know your greatness, perhaps more than you do. I see you. As for Kent…he will always be at our table.

Thank you to Dr. Ron Jenson who initiated my thinking about the true economics of goodness, and who believed in me and my ability to forge forward. Good really does beget good!

Thank you to Daniel Yeager of Nu-Image Design for making this process simple for me and for the beautiful cover design.

To my many friends, thank you for the examples of being good for Goodness Sake. I have lived and I have learned from every experience and from your collective wisdom.

I love you and I thank you. - Kristin

DISCUSSION QUESTIONS

What is your impression of:

- Ray
- Alison
- Matthew
- Madilyn
- The Host
- Braylon
- The Weeping Willow

What do you think it means to be good for goodness sake?

What are the qualities and core values that are expressed or perhaps needed by each character??

What was the role of The Host in the story?

What did you see from the Weeping Willow's eyes?

If you were the dining table at the Only B&B, what stories would you tell?

What would you say to your younger self?

What wisdom have you accumulated through the years?

How has being 'good' paid off for you with family? Friends? In business? Professionally?

How are you 'good'? What helped you become so?

Who do you need? What do you need?

If you were to tie an ornament to the limb of the Weeping Willow or some sort of leave behind, what would it be?

What does your imagination tell you happened in the Host's kitchen when few were allowed to enter?

What did you learn? Or think about? ....as you read and discussed Be Good For Goodness Sake?

ABOUT KRISTIN ANDRESS

Kristin began filling spiral notebooks with stories when she was six years old. When asked what she loves to do her simple response is, "I love to read and write." She grew up in a library where her mother worked and she spent many hours in a bean bag chair lost and transformed through stories.

Originally from the beloved small town of Pittsfield, IL, her world expanded as she was transported through books to adventures, history, art, faith, suspense, romance, and through narrative and vocabulary. Inside the pages, she developed a belief system that she could...??... And, she has completed that sentence and answered that question many times over.

Through her bachelor's and master's programs, her business endeavors, and her travels, she met and continues to meet and appreciate many people and places she views as 'studies' for her creativity. Kristin is intuitive about people and meets you where you are....and sometimes brings you to where you can or must be.

She has experienced loss of loved ones and she has loved, giving her depth of expression and experience to explore humanity and our nature. Through all, she made good and bad turns as we do, and eventually she ended up here....knowing that goodness is due to nurture and nature and often pure choice...and that good begets good.

She continues to be a student of authors. She reads.

The only intention of this book and her ensuing work is to have us truly see each other. That is where goodness starts...and continues.

Please visit www.KristinAndress.com for more information.